Oceans

Kate Riggs

seedlings

CREATIVE EDUCATION • CREATIVE PAPERBACKS

Published by Creative Education and Creative Paperbacks
P.O. Box 227, Mankato, Minnesota 56002
Creative Education and Creative Paperbacks
are imprints of The Creative Company
www.thecreativecompany.us

Design by Ellen Huber; production by Joe Kahnke
Art direction by Rita Marshall
Printed in the United States of America

Photographs by Alamy (Cultura Creative), Corbis (Wild Wonders
of Europe/Zankl/Nature Picture Library), Dreamstime (Alptraum,
Apolobay, Michal Bednarek, Richard Carey, Neacsu Razvan
Chirnoaga, Serban Enache, Feel4nature, Irochka, Sergii Koval,
Olga Kovalenko, Marina Kuznetsova, David Mckee, Steven
Melanson, Mychadre77, Vadim Petrov, Alexander Potapov, Fenkie
Sumolang, Vilainecrevette, Yarkovoy), Flickr (David A. Hofmann),
NOAA (NOAA Okeanos Explorer Program)

Library of Congress Cataloging-in-Publication Data
Riggs, Kate.
Oceans / Kate Riggs.
p. cm. — (Seedlings)
Summary: A kindergarten-level introduction to oceans,
covering their climate, plant and animal life, and such
defining features as their salty water.
Includes bibliographical references and index.
ISBN 978-1-60818-743-0 (hardcover)
ISBN 978-1-62832-339-9 (pbk)
ISBN 978-1-56660-778-0 (eBook)
1. Oceans—Juvenile literature.
GC21.5.R54 2016
551.46—dc23   2015041990
CCSS: RI.K.1, 2, 3, 4, 5, 6, 7;
RI.1.1, 2, 3, 4, 5, 6, 7; RF.K.1, 3; RF.1.1

First Edition HC 9 8 7 6 5 4 3 2 1
First Edition PBK 9 8 7 6 5 4 3 2 1

TABLE OF CONTENTS

Hello, ocean!

An ocean has salty water. Five oceans cover most of Earth.

The largest is
the Pacific.

Ocean water
always moves.
Sea turtles move
with the water.

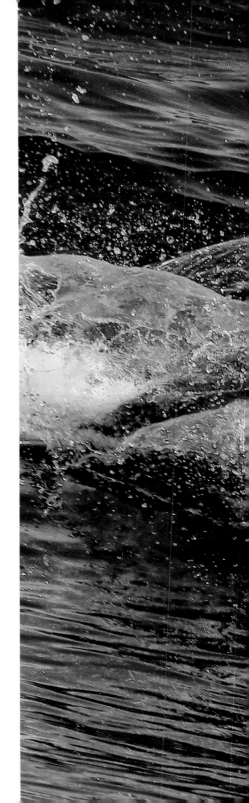

Dolphins jump above the water!

Plants grow in ocean sand and rock.

Many animals eat seaweed. Crabs hide in it.

Many fish live in the oceans. Whale sharks are the biggest fish. They like warm waters.

The oceans are deep.
Strange creatures
live down there.

The deepest part
is 36,200 feet.
This is called the
Mariana Trench.

Big waves crash on land.

Fish swim with the waves back to sea. Birds fly close to the water.

Goodbye, ocean!

Picture an Ocean

wave

shore

crab

rocks

20

below water

anemone

angelfish

clownfish

sand

21

Pacific: the biggest of Earth's oceans

seaweed: plants that grow in water but need a lot of light

trench: a long ditch in the floor of an ocean

Read More

Dawson, Emily C. *Ocean Animals.*
Mankato, Minn.: Amicus, 2011.

Riggs, Kate. *Dolphins.*
Mankato, Minn.: Creative Education, 2013.

Websites

Enchanted Learning: Ocean Crafts
http://www.enchantedlearning.com/crafts/ocean/
Make ocean animals, color pictures, and do more ocean-themed activities.

National Geographic Kids: Ocean Portal
http://kids.nationalgeographic.com/explore/ocean-portal/
Explore the oceans through games and videos.

Index

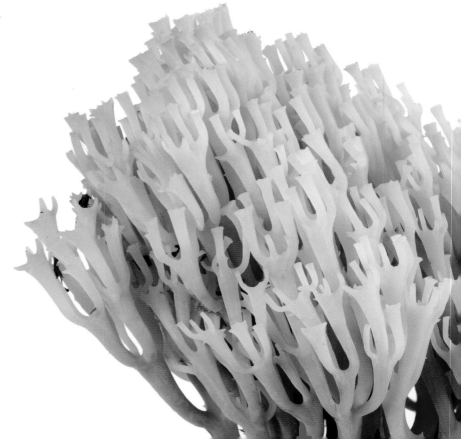